GROVER *Cleveland*

GROVER *Cleveland*

OUR TWENTY-SECOND AND TWENTY-FOURTH PRESIDENT

By Ann Graham Gaines

SPIRIT
of America™

The Child's World®, Inc.
Chanhassen, Minnesota

13

GROVER *Cleveland*

Published in the United States of America by The Child's World®, Inc.
PO Box 326 • Chanhassen, MN 55317-0326 • 800-599-READ • www.childsworld.com

Acknowledgments
The Creative Spark: Mary Francis-DeMarois, Project Director; Elizabeth Sirimarco Budd, Series Editor; Robert Court, Design and Art Direction; Janine Graham, Page Layout; Jennifer Moyers, Production

The Child's World®, Inc.: Mary Berendes, Publishing Director; Red Line Editorial, Fact Research; Cindy Klingel, Curriculum Advisor; Robert Noyed, Historical Advisor

Photos
Cover: White House Collection, courtesy White House Historical Association; courtesy Buffalo and Erie County Historical Society: 6, 8-10, 15, 16, 28, 35; courtesy Grover Cleveland Birthplace: 7 (photo by John Collins), 11 (photo restoration by Al J. Frazza), 14; Corbis: 19, 23, 26; courtesy Benjamin Harrison Home, Indianapolis, Indiana: 30; Library of Congress: 13, 18, 20, 36; North Wind Pictures: 21, 25, 29, 37; Princeton University Library: 33

Library of Congress Cataloging-in-Publication Data
Gaines, Ann.
    Grover Cleveland : our twenty second and twenty-fourth president / by Ann Graham Gaines.
        p. cm.
    Includes bibliographical references and index.
    ISBN 1-56766-859-3
    1. Cleveland, Grover, 1837–1908—Juvenile literature. 2. Presidents—United States—Biography—Juvenile literature. [1. Cleveland, Grover, 1837–1908. 2. Presidents.]   I. Title.
    E697 .G35 2001
    973.8'5'092—dc21
                                                            00-011457

23   25   31

Contents

Chapter ONE   *The Early Years*   6

Chapter TWO   *Life in Politics*   14

Chapter THREE   *The First Term*   20

Chapter FOUR   *The Second Term*   30

Time Line   38

Glossary Terms   40

Our Presidents   42

Presidential Facts   46

For Further Information   47

Index   48

The Early Years

President Grover Cleveland was known for his honesty and for his willingness to work hard. As one historian wrote, "It is as a strong man, a man of character, that Cleveland will live in history."

GROVER CLEVELAND WAS THE ONLY PRESIDENT to serve two terms that did not immediately follow one another. For the U.S. president, a term is the four-year period of time that he (or she) holds the position. Cleveland's first term began after he won the election of 1884. He lost the next presidential election in 1888. Cleveland then achieved another victory four years later, in the election of 1892.

Stephen Grover Cleveland was born on March 18, 1837, in Caldwell, New Jersey. He never used the name Stephen but was always called Grover. The Clevelands had a large and lively family. Richard and Ann Cleveland had nine children, and Grover was the fifth of them. Richard Cleveland was a Presbyterian minister. He was a friendly man, and the

GROVER CLEVELAND
BIRTHPLACE
HISTORIC SITE
DIVISION OF PARKS AND FORESTRY
STATE OF NEW JERSEY

people of his church admired him. Ann Cleveland was also well liked by the community. She helped Richard tend to his duties by visiting the sick and cooking meals for the needy. Ann also took care of her own family.

The Clevelands' home was a happy, busy place. The children played games together. They also enjoyed school. Grover Cleveland started taking classes at public school when he was six years old. He was a good student, although he was never the best in his class. He earned good grades with lots of hard work.

Stephen Grover Cleveland was born in this house in the small town of Caldwell, New Jersey. At the time, most babies were born at home, usually without help from a doctor.

Interesting Facts

▶ As a little boy, Grover Cleveland was once almost run over by a runaway horse and wagon. A passerby rescued him.

As a young teenager, Grover hoped to graduate high school and go on to college. Tragedy struck, however, and destroyed this dream. Richard Cleveland suddenly died when Grover was only 16.

By this time, the family had moved to Holland Patent, New York. Suddenly, Ann Cleveland was left alone to provide for her family. There were few jobs available for women in Holland Patent at the time, and Ann was needed at home. She still had to cook, clean, and tend to her youngest children. To help, Grover dropped out of school so he could earn money to help his family. On his own, he traveled to New York City. There he found a job at a school for the blind. He was a good teacher and found his new job interesting. But he became so homesick for his family that he soon returned to Holland Patent, where he found a different job.

At age 18, Grover left his family for good. He boarded a train intending to travel to

Ohio. But halfway through his trip, he stopped to visit relatives in Buffalo, New York. They asked him to stay for a while. His uncle hired him to work on his farm. By this time, Grover was a tall, strong man who could work for many hours at a time.

Grover liked living with his relatives and working on the farm. But when his uncle's friend offered him a job at his law office, he accepted. Grover could earn much more as a law clerk than as a farmhand. His mother still needed him to help pay the family's bills, so the increase in pay was important. Grover also enjoyed his new work. Even so, working in the law office did have one big disadvantage. It meant he sat at a desk all day long.

Soon Grover was working in the evenings as well. He had decided he wanted to become a lawyer and needed to study during every spare moment. Today most people become lawyers by attending law school. At school,

Ann Cleveland (above) was responsible for the well-being of her children after her husband died in 1853. Grover was 16 years old at the time. To help support the family, he left school to find work.

▶ The Clevelands insisted that their children be helpful and well behaved. Grover remembered being made to get out of a warm bed late at night when he forgot to hang up his clothes. Sometimes he had to help his family when he'd rather have been out having fun. Grover remembered rocking a younger sister to sleep when he really wanted to go sleigh riding.

As a young man in Buffalo, Grover Cleveland was slim, strong, and handsome. He enjoyed food a great deal, however. By the time he was president, he weighed more than 250 pounds. Later his relatives nick-named him "Uncle Jumbo" after an elephant in P. T. Barnum's circus.

10

they prepare to take the bar exam, which one must pass to become a lawyer. But Grover Cleveland could not go to law school because he did not have a high school diploma or a college degree. Instead, he had to teach himself the law. He spent all his free time studying for the bar exam. Spending many hours every day and night at his desk meant he had little exercise. Grover had always loved to eat and drink, but he also had been physically active, too. Without exercise, he began to gain weight.

This rare photograph shows Cleveland with all his brothers and sisters except one sister, who was not present for the photograph. Grover Cleveland is seated at far left.

11

▶ A neighbor's hen kept laying eggs in the Clevelands' yard. Grover felt they did not belong to his family, so he always returned them.

▶ When he was 17, Grover Cleveland was offered a full scholarship to a Presbyterian college. This would have paid for his education to become a minister like his father. Grover longed for an education, but he could not take advantage of this opportunity. His family needed him to earn money to help support them.

In 1859, thanks to hard work and determination, Grover passed the bar exam and became a lawyer. He accepted a new job in the same law office where he had worked as a clerk. Soon the people of Buffalo noticed that he did excellent work. In 1863, Grover was **appointed** assistant district attorney for Erie County, New York. This meant he was one of the lawyers who worked for the county. He took evidence collected by sheriffs and their deputies. He then went to court and tried to prove that people accused of crimes were guilty.

Grover was now a government employee. This new job made him begin to think about a career in politics, the work of the government. He joined the Democratic Party, which is one of the two most powerful **political parties** in the country. (The Republican Party is the other.) By this time, he had begun to form his own beliefs about how the government should be run. All his life, Grover Cleveland would believe that government should interfere as little as possible in the lives of the American people. He also thought people should not depend too much on the government for help.

CLEVELAND HAD JUST BEGUN TO EARN A REPUTATION AS A GOOD LAWYER when the Civil War began in 1861. The **Union** army needed many new soldiers. At first, thousands of men like those shown below volunteered to fight. But as the war continued, fewer people volunteered. The country started to draft soldiers. This means it could require young men of a certain age to join the army.

At the time, the law allowed a man to pay someone to serve in his place. In other words, he could find a substitute. Some men hired substitutes because their families depended on them. Others did so because they had important jobs. When Grover Cleveland received a message saying he had been drafted, he hired a substitute. He did not want to interrupt his successful career to become a soldier. Even more important, his family still depended on him. Cleveland paid another man to take his place, which allowed him to continue working as a lawyer.

Chapter TWO

Life in Politics

Cleveland won his first election in 1871, when he became sheriff of Erie County, New York. In this position, he became well known for his honesty.

IN 1865, GROVER CLEVELAND RAN FOR election to the office of district attorney. He did not win and left the government to work in a private law office. He stayed at that job for six years. Then, in 1871, he won his first election and became the Erie County sheriff. He investigated crimes and arrested people who broke the law. He was in charge of the county jail as well. Sheriff Cleveland could be called to a crime scene at any hour of the day or night. From time to time, he faced dangerous criminals.

In 1873, Cleveland's term as sheriff ended. He returned to practicing law. Over the years, he became well known to the people of Buffalo. He was known for being honest, firm, kind, and hardworking. He devoted a great deal of time and energy to every job he held.

In 1881, the people of Buffalo elected Cleveland their mayor. This was a difficult job, and he faced many challenges. City officials had not always been honest in the past. Some had cheated the city government out of money. Others had appointed their friends and relations to city jobs instead of choosing the best people with the most skills. As mayor, Cleveland was in favor of **reform.** This meant he wanted to improve the way the city was run. He planned to make sure Buffalo's workers were honest. There would be no wrongdoing in the government with Grover Cleveland in

Cleveland traveled to Buffalo after his father died. He remained in the city for the next 28 years, winning increasingly important positions in the city's government.

Interesting Facts

▶ From the time he first arrived in Buffalo, Cleveland was interested in politics. During elections, he would walk around town reminding people to vote.

15

FOR GOVERNOR,

Grover Cleveland,

OF

BUFFALO, N.Y.

As governor of New York, Cleveland made sure that the state government used its money wisely. During this time, he won such a widespread reputation for honesty that the Democratic Party wanted him to run for president.

charge. Such honesty won the respect of other people working for government reform, including officials in the New York State government. Leaders of the state's Democratic Party soon asked Cleveland to run for an even more important office. In 1882, he ran for governor of New York State.

Cleveland won the election. The following January, he moved to Albany, the state capital, to take the position. As governor, he continued to win praise for his dedication to reform. He fought to stop **corruption** in the state government and in New York City. By nature, Cleveland was frugal, meaning he did not like to waste money. He refused to sign **bills** that he felt were a waste of the state's money. He was also stubborn and fought hard for what he thought was right. Both of these traits helped Cleveland fight dishonesty and overspending in New York's state government.

While he was governor, the people of New York learned more about the honest **politician** from Buffalo. They admired Cleveland's accomplishments, but few people outside of New York had ever heard of him. Even so, leaders in the Democratic Party asked Cleveland to run for president in 1884. They thought he was an ideal **candidate,** one who could win votes not only from his own political party, the Democrats, but also from the rival party, the Republicans.

Why would Republicans vote for a Democratic candidate? Because members of the Republican Party were split into two groups. One of these groups was made up of reformers like Cleveland. They called themselves Mugwumps, an Indian word meaning "war leader." They were unhappy with the corruption in the Republican Party. Democrats hoped that with Cleveland as their candidate, Mugwumps would vote for him rather than for a Republican.

This cartoon shows Grover Cleveland as a fisherman, "landing" the presidency, as his opponent, James Blaine, looks on. Cleveland won the election of 1884 and became president the following March.

THE GREAT NATIONAL FISHING MATCH.

IT'S MINE?

"THE RESULT."

But it proved harder for Cleveland to win the election than anyone had expected. In the middle of the campaign, a newspaper reported that Cleveland was the father of a young, unmarried woman's child. Many Americans refused to vote for him because of this. (Today historians believe that he was probably not the child's father. But Cleveland never denied the charges, perhaps because he wanted to protect one of his friends.) But Cleveland's opponent, James G. Blaine, had a bad reputation. As a member of Congress, Blaine had been accused of illegal activities. The election was a nasty one, with members of each political party saying terrible things about the other's candidate. On Election Day of 1884, Grover Cleveland won by a small number of votes. After a tough campaign, he was on his way to Washington, D.C.

18

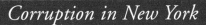

IN THE 1870S AND 1880S, THERE was corruption in the New York State government. Some dishonest officials used their power to earn money for themselves. The situation was especially bad in New York City, where William Marcy Tweed (left) had become the "boss."

Tweed was a member of the city council. He was also the leader of Tammany Hall, an organization that helped **immigrants.** Tammany Hall found jobs and homes for people who had just arrived in the United States. But it also tried to control New York City's government. Tammany Hall paid people to use more than one name to cast extra votes in elections. This way, Boss Tweed could make sure the people he supported were elected to office.

Tweed and other government officials also helped their friends find work. If the government had to hire builders, for example, these officials made sure their friends received the jobs. In exchange, the officials demanded a portion of what the government paid the builders for their work. Once Boss Tweed helped a man get a contract to work on a city building. Although it was not a big job, Tweed's friend charged close to two million dollars. Much of that money went into Tweed's own pocket. As governor of New York, Grover Cleveland fought hard to end such corruption. Along the way, he angered many people in the New York government.

Chapter THREE

The First Term

When Cleveland became president, few Americans knew who he was. One challenge he faced was earning the respect of lawmakers in Congress.

CLEVELAND'S **INAUGURATION** TOOK PLACE ON March 4, 1885. He moved into the White House and set to work at once. Cleveland became one of the hardest-working presidents of all time. Many days he spent more than 12 hours working at his desk. Sometimes he started work at eight o'clock in the morning and did not stop until after eight o'clock at night.

As president, Cleveland continued working for reform in government. He enforced the Pendleton Civil Service Act. This law had been passed when Chester A. Arthur was president. It put in place a "merit system" for government workers. This meant that government jobs could be given only to people who were qualified for them. Politicians could no longer hire people simply because they owed them favors.

When Cleveland arrived in Washington for his inauguration, it was only his second visit to the nation's capital city. The crowd that gathered for the event was the largest he had ever seen.

For one thing, they could not offer jobs to people who had given them money to spend on an election campaign.

Cleveland went through the lists of employees who worked for the national government.

▸ When Americans elected Cleveland in 1884, he became the first Democrat to win a presidential election since James Buchanan in 1856. One reason for this was that many southerners were Democrats. For years, people in the North blamed southern Democrats for the Civil War.

▸ When he first became president, Cleveland did not have a secretary. He sometimes answered the White House telephone himself.

He fired those who had gotten their jobs unfairly. This angered many members of Congress. One half of Congress, the Senate, had the right to accept or decline any person the president chose for a position. To show their anger, senators refused to accept the people Cleveland chose. They claimed that filling jobs was not one of the president's duties. Cleveland showed his stubborn side and fought back. He pointed out that the U.S. **Constitution** gives the president power to fill government positions.

The American public supported Cleveland. The Senate finally gave in and started to approve the people he chose for government jobs. In 1886, Congress voted to overturn the Tenure of Office Act. This 1867 law had limited the power presidents had to appoint or fire government officials. When it was overturned, it was a victory for Cleveland.

Cleveland had become a powerful president. But he never offered his opinion about lawmaking to Congress. He did not suggest ideas for new laws, nor did he discuss bills with members of Congress. If he approved of a bill, he signed it into law. When he did not

like a bill, he vetoed it. When a president vetoes a bill, he refuses to sign it. This means it does not become a law. Cleveland vetoed hundreds of bills. They would not become law unless two-thirds of Congress voted to **overrule** his veto.

A political cartoon shows Cleveland shaking hands with an ordinary citizen. Although the president often had difficulty working with Congress, he was popular with the American people.

Most often, Cleveland vetoed spending bills. During his presidency, Congress passed hundreds of bills providing **pensions** to Civil War soldiers. Cleveland read every one carefully and then vetoed almost all of them. He knew that many people who applied for these pensions were dishonest. Some had left the army without permission. Others had never even served in the army.

Cleveland looked for other ways to make the government spend less money. One way was to pay his own expenses. Earlier, the government had paid for many of the presidents' activities. It provided a luxurious sailboat for their use, which Cleveland refused. He also turned down other benefits that presidents had enjoyed in the past.

In 1886, Cleveland surprised the nation by announcing his plans to marry. He was then 49 years old. His bride-to-be, Frances Folsom, was just 21. Cleveland had known Frances since she was a baby. When she was 12, her father had died. He had been Cleveland's friend and law partner. His **will** said he wanted Cleveland to be Frances's guardian. Frances lived with Cleveland for six years before he sent her away to college.

When Frances turned 21, Cleveland wrote asking for her hand in marriage. She accepted, and then went to Europe for a long tour. When she returned, their engagement was announced to the public. Five days later, they were married in the White House. They invited only a few friends and celebrated in a very quiet manner. In keeping with his penny-

Cleveland married Frances Folsom on June 2, 1886. Only about 30 guests attended the event, including Cleveland's closest assistants and the couple's friends and family.

In 1886, France gave the United States a beautiful gift: the Statue of Liberty. President Cleveland dedicated the statue in front of a large, excited crowd that had gathered for the event.

pinching nature, Cleveland had not wanted his wedding to cost very much. He did make one very romantic gesture, however. He made sure the White House was filled with beautiful flowers.

After their marriage, Grover and Frances Cleveland went on a five-day honeymoon to Maryland. When they returned to Washington, they settled into a quiet life. Cleveland continued to save the government every penny he could. He even discouraged the White House cook from making fancy meals.

Toward the end of his first term, President Cleveland asked Congress to lower **tariffs.** President Lincoln had increased these taxes, which were placed on **imports** to help pay for the Civil War. After the war, they protected U.S. companies because they increased the price of foreign goods. Cleveland thought high tariffs were no longer needed. He pointed out that the government had a great deal of money. He believed that Congress used the extra money to fund unnecessary projects. But Cleveland received little support for his plan. Owners of big businesses complained. So did workers, who believed that tariffs helped keep their wages high because more American goods were sold. As the next election approached, President Cleveland was losing popularity.

At age 21, Frances Cleveland was the youngest first lady in history. She was also one of the most popular. Americans admired her grace and beauty. One member of the White House staff said, "Her very presence threw an air of beauty on the entire surroundings, whatever the occasion or company."

THE U.S. CONSTITUTION GIVES PRESIDENTS THE RIGHT TO VETO ANY BILL passed by Congress. This means that the president can refuse to sign a bill, and it will not become a law. If this happens, the bill is sent back to Congress. Both the House of Representatives and the Senate, the two parts of Congress, must vote on it again. If less than two-thirds of Congress vote in favor of the bill, it "dies." This means it does not become a law.

Early presidents like George Washington knew they had the right to veto, but they rarely did so. The presidents' use of the veto increased over time, however. Andrew Jackson used it 12 times. Ulysses S. Grant vetoed more than 90 bills. Grover Cleveland vetoed a total of 584 bills, most of them small pension bills.

Chapter FOUR

The Second Term

Benjamin Harrison (above) won the election of 1888. His inauguration took place on March 4, 1889, a cold and rainy day. Grover Cleveland held an umbrella over Harrison's head as he took the oath of office.

IN 1888, PRESIDENT CLEVELAND RAN FOR reelection, and he expected to win. But his stand on high tariffs caused him to lose many votes. The Republican Party chose Benjamin Harrison as their candidate. He was a hero from the Civil War and the grandson of William Henry Harrison, the ninth president. Benjamin Harrison's campaign favored tariffs. Workers and American businesses supported him.

In November, Grover Cleveland actually won more popular votes, which are votes cast by the American public. But Cleveland lost the electoral vote, which actually determines who wins a presidential election. Electoral votes are cast by representatives of the American public. Each state chooses representatives who vote for a candidate in an election. These representatives

30

vote according to what the majority of people in their state want. But representatives from Cleveland's own state, New York, did not vote for him. They were still angry about his attempts to reform their state government.

Shocked and disappointed at his loss, Grover and Frances Cleveland left Washington right after Benjamin Harrison's inauguration. They moved to New York City, where Cleveland practiced law. During that time, the Clevelands had their first child, a little girl named Ruth. They would have five children together.

This campaign poster for President Grover Cleveland tells of his plan to lower tariffs, which are taxes placed on goods from other countries. Cleveland's opinion that tariffs should be lowered cost him the election of 1888.

Harrison proved to be a weak president. He accomplished little during his term. Democrats realized that they missed Cleveland. They chose him as their candidate once more. In 1892, Cleveland faced Harrison in another

31

▶ When the Clevelands left the White House in 1889, Mrs. Cleveland asked a servant to take good care of the furniture and decorations. "I want to find everything just as it is now when we come back again," she said. Surprised, the servant asked when she expected to return. "We are coming back just four years from today," she replied.

▶ Frances Cleveland was very popular with the American public. Some advertisers began to use her name and picture to advertise products such as cosmetics, soap, and medicine. Unfortunately, they did so without her permission.

election. At first, it looked as though it would be a close race. But toward the end of the campaign, Harrison's wife became very ill. She died just two weeks before Election Day. By that time, Harrison did not care how the election turned out, and he stopped campaigning. In the end, he lost to Cleveland by a large number of votes.

Cleveland's second term was very difficult. Just two months after his inauguration, a **depression** began. Companies went out of business, and workers lost their jobs. Many Americans suddenly became poor. Cleveland tried to help end the depression, but he failed.

During the first year of his second term, Cleveland suffered a personal crisis as well. His doctor told him that he had developed cancer in his mouth. He had a **tumor** that needed to be removed. Cleveland did not want Americans to know he had cancer. He made arrangements to have a surgeon remove the tumor in secret. He sneaked away from the White House to a friend's boat. The surgery was performed there. The operation was a success, and the tumor was removed. But to do so, the surgeon also had to remove a large portion of his upper jaw. Cleveland had it replaced with an artificial rubber jaw, which made it difficult for him to speak. It took months for him to learn to speak clearly again.

Two important events took place during Cleveland's second term. Earlier, the Senate had voted to make the islands of Hawaii part of the United States. An agreement had already been written, but Cleveland did not

President Cleveland's second term was filled with difficult challenges. By the end, he had no interest in seeking another four years in office.

▶ Grover Cleveland was a very heavy smoker. He especially enjoyed smoking cigars. This bad habit finally caught up with him when doctors discovered he had cancer of the mouth.

▶ Because Cleveland insisted that doctors treat his cancer in secret, Americans did not learn of it until 1917, nine years after his death.

▶ Toward the end of his presidency, Grover Cleveland became so unpopular that he ordered the White House gates locked to keep out angry Americans.

think the United States had a right to take over Hawaii. He refused to sign the agreement. Because of Cleveland, Hawaii would not become a U.S. **territory** until 1900. It finally became the 50th state in 1959.

In 1894, Cleveland used his presidential power yet again. He sent soldiers to end the Pullman **strike** in Chicago. Workers were demanding better treatment from the Pullman Car Company. Cleveland's decision to end the strike made him unpopular with American workers. They felt he had sided with rich business owners. In congressional elections that fall, Republicans won many seats in the Senate and the House. After that, Cleveland no longer had the tremendous power he once enjoyed.

Americans lost faith in Cleveland as his second term wore on. He decided not to run in the next election. He simply did not want the job anymore. Cleveland left office in 1897 and retired in Princeton, New Jersey.

Even in retirement, Cleveland remained in the public eye. He wrote books and articles and made speeches. He did a great deal of work for Princeton University, raising funds and speaking to students. But, after years of nonstop work, he also let himself take time off to relax. He spent time with Frances and their children. He also enjoyed two of his favorite pastimes, fishing and hunting.

In his late 60s, Cleveland slowed down. He continued to have health problems. He finally died at his home on June 24, 1908, at the age of 71. The nation mourned his death. Today many Americans consider Cleveland to have been a fine president, admired for his honesty, dedication, and hard work.

After Cleveland's presidency, he and his family moved to Princeton, New Jersey. Shown in this photograph (from left to right) are Esther, Francis, Mrs. Frances Cleveland, Marion, Richard, and Grover Cleveland. Their first child, Ruth, had died of a serious illness.

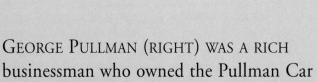

GEORGE PULLMAN (RIGHT) WAS A RICH
businessman who owned the Pullman Car
Company, located near Chicago. It made railroad cars to carry passengers.
Train travel became very popular after the transcontinental railroad was
finished in 1869. Pullman sleeping cars were fancy and comfortable.
They included seats that turned into beds. Additional beds pulled
down from the ceiling. Other features of Pullman cars included beautiful
wood panels, huge mirrors, and thick, soft carpets.

The Pullman Car Company employed many workers. Mr. Pullman
built a town just for them. This was what was known as a company town.
Mr. Pullman provided workers with schools, parks, a store, and a library—
but he also set many rules. Many workers became dissatisfied living there.
They became especially angry after Mr. Pullman cut their wages but did
not lower their rent.

Thousands of his workers joined the American Railway Union and
went on strike. Unions are groups of workers who band together to demand
better wages or improved working conditions. Soon, about 120,000 workers
were on strike. Although the strike remained peaceful, it stopped nearly all
rail traffic.

Finally, the U.S. government ordered the union to make its members
go back to work. When the union refused, President Cleveland sent thousands of soldiers to take care of the problem. When the troops arrived,
union members rioted. As the violence grew serious, soldiers attacked the

workers. In the end, 13 people died, and more than 50 were wounded. The union gave in and called off the strike. Workers were forced to return to work.

Although the soldiers ended the strike, it caused serious problems in the workforce. The decision to send troops angered many working Americans. They believed that the U.S. government and wealthy business owners were working together to enslave poor Americans.

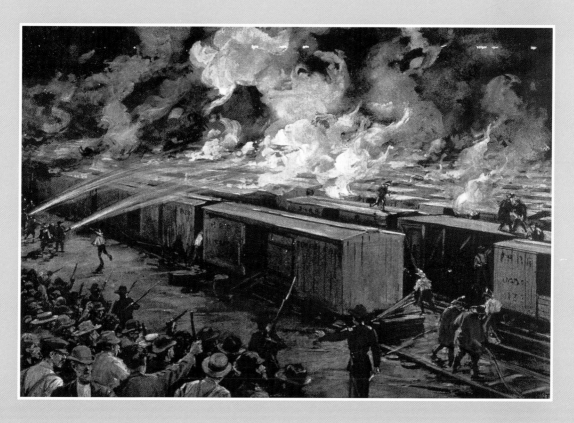

1837 Grover Cleveland is born on March 18 in Caldwell, New Jersey.

1843 Cleveland starts school at age six.

1853 Cleveland drops out of high school to help support his family after his father dies.

1855 Cleveland settles in Buffalo, New York. He works on his uncle's farm and then in a lawyer's office as a clerk.

1859 Cleveland passes the bar exam and becomes a lawyer.

1861 The Civil War begins. Grover Cleveland is drafted into the Union army but hires a substitute to fight in his place.

1863 Grover Cleveland becomes an assistant district attorney for Erie County, New York.

1865 Grover Cleveland loses his first election when he runs for the office of district attorney.

1871 Grover Cleveland is elected sheriff of Erie County.

1873 Cleveland's term as sheriff ends. He goes back to work as an attorney in a law office.

1881 Cleveland is elected mayor of Buffalo, New York.

1882 After only one year as mayor of Buffalo, Cleveland is elected governor of New York.

1883 Cleveland begins his duties as governor of New York.

1884 Cleveland is elected president of the United States.

1885 In March, Cleveland is inaugurated president and begins his duties. During his first year in office, he fights with Congress over who should fill government positions.

1886 Congress admits that Cleveland has the right to make appointments to political office and overturns the Tenure of Office Act. This represents an important victory for Cleveland. Cleveland marries Frances Folsom in the White House on June 2.

1887 Cleveland becomes involved in a fight with Congress over high tariffs. He wants them reduced, but business leaders and workers do not.

1888 Cleveland runs for reelection. He is shocked when he loses. His stand on tariffs is the major cause for the loss.

1889 Benjamin Harrison is sworn in as the new president. Grover and Frances Cleveland move to New York City. He returns to work as an attorney.

1892 Cleveland runs for president a third time. He beats his opponent, Benjamin Harrison, who had defeated him four years earlier.

1893 Cleveland begins his second term as president. A depression begins. Many businesses close, and people lose their jobs. Although the government wants to make Hawaii a U.S. territory, Cleveland refuses to agree. Cleveland is diagnosed with cancer of the mouth, and a tumor is removed in secret.

1894 Cleveland exerts his presidential power and sends American troops to end the Pullman strike. This makes him unpopular with the public. In the fall election, Republicans are elected to many seats in Congress, replacing Democrats. Cleveland loses much of his power after the elections.

1896 Cleveland decides not to run for a third term as president. William McKinley is elected the 25th president.

1897 After McKinley is inaugurated, Cleveland retires to private life.

1908 After more than 10 years in retirement, Grover Cleveland dies at home on June 24 at the age of 71.

appoint (uh-POINT)
When people are appointed, they are asked by an important official to fill a position. Cleveland was appointed assistant district attorney of Erie County.

bills (BILZ)
Bills are ideas for new laws that are presented to a group of lawmakers. Cleveland refused to sign bills that he felt were a waste of the government's money.

campaign (kam-PAYN)
A campaign is the process of running for an election, including activities such as giving speeches or attending rallies. Cleveland won the election of 1884 after a tough campaign.

candidate (KAN-dih-det)
A candidate is a person running in an election. Members of the Democratic Party thought Cleveland would make an excellent presidential candidate in 1884.

constitution (kon-stih-TOO-shun)
A constitution is the set of basic principles that govern a state, country, or society. The U.S. Constitution gives the president the power to fill government positions.

corruption (kuh-RUP-shun)
Corruption is dishonesty. Cleveland fought corruption in the government.

depression (deh-PRESH-un)
A depression is a period of time in which there is little business activity, and many people are out of work. A depression began shortly after Cleveland entered office in 1893.

immigrants (IM-ih-grentz)
Immigrants are people who move to a new country. Tammany Hall was a New York organization that helped immigrants find work.

imports (IM-portz)
Imports are goods brought from one country to another. Cleveland felt that higher taxes on imports were not needed.

inauguration (ih-nawg-yuh-RAY-shun)
An inauguration is the ceremony that takes place when a new president begins a term. Cleveland's first inauguration took place March 4, 1885.

overrule (oh-ver-ROOL)
If Congress votes to overrule, it does not accept a president's veto. For a bill to become law, two-thirds of both houses of Congress must vote to overrule the veto.

pensions (PEN-shunz)
Pensions are regular payments made to someone who is retired. The government paid pensions to soldiers who fought in the Civil War.

**political parties
(puh-LIT-ih-kul PAR-teez)**
Political parties are groups of people who share similar ideas about how to run a government. The Democratic Party is one of the two most powerful political parties in the United States.

politician (pawl-ih-TISH-un)
A politician is a person who holds an office in government. Cleveland was a politician.

reform (ree-FORM)
Reform is change that improves something. Cleveland wanted to reform the way the government was run.

strike (STRYK)
A strike is when workers quit work-ing hoping to force an employer to meet a demand. Workers at the Pullman Car Company went on strike to ask for better wages.

tariffs (TAIR-ifs)
Tariffs are taxes on goods that are imported from other countries. Cleveland wanted to lower tariffs.

territory (TAIR-uh-tor-ee)
A territory is a land or region, especially land that belongs to a government. Cleveland did not want Hawaii to become a U.S. territory.

tumor (TOO-mur)
A tumor is a growth of cells or tissue in the body that is not normal. Cleveland had a tumor in his mouth.

Union (YOON-yen)
The Union is another name for the United States of America. During the Civil War, the North was called the Union. A Union can also be a group of workers who have banded together to demand better wages or improved working conditions.

will (WILL)
A will is a set of instructions that states what should be done with a person's things when he or she dies. Cleveland's law partner left instructions in his will regarding Frances Folsom.

President	Birthplace	Life Span	Presidency	Political Party	First Lady
George Washington	Virginia	1732–1799	1789–1797	None	Martha Dandridge Custis Washington
John Adams	Massachusetts	1735–1826	1797–1801	Federalist	Abigail Smith Adams
Thomas Jefferson	Virginia	1743–1826	1801–1809	Democratic-Republican	widower
James Madison	Virginia	1751–1836	1809–1817	Democratic Republican	Dolley Payne Todd Madison
James Monroe	Virginia	1758–1831	1817–1825	Democratic Republican	Elizabeth Kortright Monroe
John Quincy Adams	Massachusetts	1767–1848	1825–1829	Democratic-Republican	Louisa Johnson Adams
Andrew Jackson	South Carolina	1767–1845	1829–1837	Democrat	widower
Martin Van Buren	New York	1782–1862	1837–1841	Democrat	widower
William H. Harrison	Virginia	1773–1841	1841	Whig	Anna Symmes Harrison
John Tyler	Virginia	1790–1862	1841–1845	Whig	Letitia Christian Tyler / Julia Gardiner Tyler
James K. Polk	North Carolina	1795–1849	1845–1849	Democrat	Sarah Childress Polk

Our PRESIDENTS

President	Birthplace	Life Span	Presidency	Political Party	First Lady
Zachary Taylor	Virginia	1784–1850	1849–1850	Whig	Margaret Mackall Smith Taylor
Millard Fillmore	New York	1800–1874	1850–1853	Whig	Abigail Powers Fillmore
Franklin Pierce	New Hampshire	1804–1869	1853–1857	Democrat	Jane Means Appleton Pierce
James Buchanan	Pennsylvania	1791–1868	1857–1861	Democrat	never married
Abraham Lincoln	Kentucky	1809–1865	1861–1865	Republican	Mary Todd Lincoln
Andrew Johnson	North Carolina	1808–1875	1865–1869	Democrat	Eliza McCardle Johnson
Ulysses S. Grant	Ohio	1822–1885	1869–1877	Republican	Julia Dent Grant
Rutherford B. Hayes	Ohio	1822–1893	1877–1881	Republican	Lucy Webb Hayes
James A. Garfield	Ohio	1831–1881	1881	Republican	Lucretia Rudolph Garfield
Chester A. Arthur	Vermont	1829–1886	1881–1885	Republican	widower
Grover Cleveland	New Jersey	1837–1908	1885–1889	Democrat	Frances Folsom Cleveland

President	Birthplace	Life Span	Presidency	Political Party	First Lady
Benjamin Harrison	Ohio	1833–1901	1889–1893	Republican	Caroline Scott Harrison
Grover Cleveland	New Jersey	1837–1908	1893–1897	Democrat	Frances Folsom Cleveland
William McKinley	Ohio	1843–1901	1897–1901	Republican	Ida Saxton McKinley
Theodore Roosevelt	New York	1858–1919	1901–1909	Republican	Edith Kermit Carow Roosevelt
William H. Taft	Ohio	1857–1930	1909–1913	Republican	Helen Herron Taft
Woodrow Wilson	Virginia	1856–1924	1913–1921	Democrat	Ellen L. Axson Wilson Edith Bolling Galt Wilson
Warren G. Harding	Ohio	1865–1923	1921–1923	Republican	Florence Kling De Wolfe Harding
Calvin Coolidge	Vermont	1872–1933	1923–1929	Republican	Grace Goodhue Coolidge
Herbert C. Hoover	Iowa	1874–1964	1929–1933	Republican	Lou Henry Hoover
Franklin D. Roosevelt	New York	1882–1945	1933–1945	Democrat	Anna Eleanor Roosevelt Roosevelt
Harry S. Truman	Missouri	1884–1972	1945–1953	Democrat	Elizabeth Wallace Truman

Our PRESIDENTS

President	Birthplace	Life Span	Presidency	Political Party	First Lady
Dwight D. Eisenhower	Texas	1890–1969	1953–1961	Republican	Mary "Mamie" Doud Eisenhower
John F. Kennedy	Massachusetts	1917–1963	1961–1963	Democrat	Jacqueline Bouvier Kennedy
Lyndon B. Johnson	Texas	1908–1973	1963–1969	Democrat	Claudia Alta Taylor Johnson
Richard M. Nixon	California	1913–1994	1969–1974	Republican	Thelma Catherine Ryan Nixon
Gerald Ford	Nebraska	1913–	1974–1977	Republican	Elizabeth "Betty" Bloomer Warren Ford
James Carter	Georgia	1924–	1977–1981	Democrat	Rosalynn Smith Carter
Ronald Reagan	Illinois	1911–	1981–1989	Republican	Nancy Davis Reagan
George Bush	Massachusetts	1924–	1989–1993	Republican	Barbara Pierce Bush
William Clinton	Arkansas	1946–	1993–2001	Democrat	Hillary Rodham Clinton
George W. Bush	Connecticut	1946–	2001–	Republican	Laura Welch Bush

Presidential FACTS

Qualifications
To run for president, a candidate must
- be at least 35 years old
- be a citizen who was born in the United States
- have lived in the United States for 14 years

Term of Office
A president's term of office is four years. No president can stay in office for more than two terms.

Election Date
The presidential election takes place every four years on the first Tuesday of November.

Inauguration Date
Presidents are inaugurated on January 20.

Oath of Office
I do solemnly swear I will faithfully execute the office of the President of the United States and will to the best of my ability preserve, protect, and defend the Constitution of the United States.

Write a Letter to the President
One of the best things about being a U.S. citizen is that Americans get to participate in their government. They can speak out if they feel government leaders aren't doing their jobs. They can also praise leaders who are going the extra mile. Do you have something you'd like the president to do? Should the president worry more about the environment and encourage people to recycle? Should the government spend more money on our schools? You can write a letter to the president to say how you feel!

1600 Pennsylvania Avenue
Washington, D.C. 20500

You can even send an e-mail to: president@whitehouse.gov

For Further INFORMATION

Internet Sites

See an excellent Web site devoted to Grover Cleveland created by a high school student (Josh Smith of Santa Barbara, California):
http://www.rain.org/%Eturnpike/grover/Main.html

Read a short biography of Grover Cleveland:
http://www.whitehouse.gov/WH/glimpse/presidents/html/gc22.html

Visit Grover Cleveland's birthplace:
http://www.caldwellnj.com/grover.htm

Learn more about Grover Cleveland when he taught at a school for the blind:
http://www.nyise.org/history/grover.htm

Find out more about Frances Folsom Cleveland:
http://www1.whitehouse.govv/WH/glimpse/firstladies/tml/fc24.html

See cartoons of Cleveland published during the 1900 presidential campaign:
http://www.history.ohio.state.edu/projects/uscartoons/Cleveland1900.htm

Read some of Cleveland's own words:
http://www.americanpresident.org/KoTrain/Courses/GC/GC_In_His_Own_Words

Learn more about all the presidents and visit the White House:
http://www.whitehouse.gov/WH/glimpse/presidents/html/presidents.html
http://www.thepresidency.org/presinfo.htm
http://www.americanpresidents.org/

Books

Cleveland, Grover. *Good Citizenship*. Bedford, MA: Applewood Books, 1996.

Francis, Sandra. *Benjamin Harrison: Our Twenty-Third President*. Chanhassen, MN: The Child's World, 2002.

Hakim, Joy. *Reconstruction and Reform*. New York: Oxford University Press, 1999.

Kent, Zachary. *Grover Cleveland*. Chicago: Childrens Press, 1988.

Index

Arthur, Chester A., 20

bills, vetoes of, 16, 22-24, 29
Blaine, James, 18
Buchanan, James, 22

Civil War, 13, 22, 27, 38
Civil War substitutes, 13, 38
Cleveland, Ann, 6-9
Cleveland, Frances Folsom, 24-25, 27-28,
   31-32, 35, 38-39
Cleveland, Richard, 6-8
Cleveland, Ruth, 31, 35
Cleveland, Stephen Grover
  as assistant district attorney, 12, 38
  birth of, 6-7, 38
  cancer of, 32, 34, 39
  cost-saving efforts, 24, 27
  death of, 35, 39
  education of, 7, 38
  farm experience, 9, 38
  as governor of New York, 16-17, 38
  honesty of, 6, 14-17, 35
  inauguration of, 20-21, 38
  law career, 12, 14, 31, 38-39
  as law clerk, 9, 38
  law studies of, 9, 11, 38
  marriage of, 24-25, 27, 38
  as mayor of Buffalo, 15, 38
  popularity of, 23, 28, 34, 39
  as president, first term, 18-21, 38
  as president, second term, 33-34, 39
  retirement of, 34-35, 39
  as sheriff of Erie County, 14, 38
  support of family, 8-9, 12-13, 38
  teaching career, 8
  weight problem, 10-11
  company towns, 36
Congress, Republican majority in, 34, 39
corruption, 16-17, 19

Democratic Party, 12, 16-17, 22, 31, 39
depression, 32, 39

electoral votes, 30-31

Folsom, Frances. *See* Cleveland, Frances Folsom
France, 26

government workers, 20-22, 38
Grant, Ulysses S., 29

Harrison, Benjamin, 30-32, 39
Harrison, William Henry, 30
Hawaii, 33-34, 39

immigrants, 19
imported products, 27

Jackson, Andrew, 29

Lincoln, Abraham, 27

McKinley, William, 39
Mugwumps, 17

Pendleton Civil Service Act, 20
pensions, 24
popular votes, 30
Pullman, George, 36
Pullman Car Company, 36
Pullman strike, 34, 36-37, 39

reforms, 15-17, 20
Republican Party, 12, 17, 34, 39

Statue of Liberty, 26

Tammany Hall, 19
tariffs, 27-28, 30-31, 39
Tenure of Office Act of 1867, 22, 38
train travel, 36
Tweed, William Marcy, 19

Union army, 13, 38

Washington, George, 29
workers, 36, 39